MW00629727

THE TRUTH ABOUT
OUR AMERICAN BIRTHS

THE TRUTH ABOUT
OUR AMERICAN BIRTHS

poems by

JUDITH SKILLMAN

Shanti Arts Publishing
Brunswick, Maine

THE TRUTH ABOUT OUR AMERICAN BIRTHS

Copyright © 2020 Judith Skillman

All Rights Reserved
No part of this book may be used or reproduced
in any manner whatsoever without the
written permission of the publisher.

Published by Shanti Arts Publishing

Shanti Arts LLC
193 Hillside Road
Brunswick, Maine 04011
shantiarts.com

Interior and cover design by Shanti Arts Designs

Cover image: Frederick Childe Hassam, *Rocky
Beach, Appledore*, 1913. Oil on canvas. Private
collection. Wikimedia Commons. Public domain.

Printed in the United States of America

ISBN: 978-1-951651-26-8 (softcover)

Library of Congress Control Number: 2020936772

for my children and grands—
Lisa, Drew, Jocelyn, Hazel, Klara, Luke, and Cedar

OTHER TITLES BY JUDITH SKILLMAN

Came Home to Winter, Deerbrook Editions, 2019

Premise of Light, Tebot Bach, 2018

Kafka's Shadow, Deerbrook Editions, 2017

Angles of Separation, Glass Lyre Press, 2015

House of Burnt Offerings, Pleasure Boat Studio, 2014

The Phoenix: New & Selected Poems, Dream Horse Press, 2014

Broken Lines—The Art and Craft of Poetry, Lummox Press 2013

The White Cypress, Červená Barva Press, 2011

The Never, Dream Horse Press, 2010

Prisoner of the Swifts, Ahadada Books, 2009

Heat Lightning: New and Selected Poems, Silverfish Review Press, 2006

Circe's Island, Silverfish Review Press, 2003

Red Town, Silverfish Review Press, 2001

Storm, Blue Begonia Press, 1998

Beethoven and the Birds, Blue Begonia Press, 1996

Worship of the Visible Spectrum, Breitenbush Books, 1988

"In the night of the falling leaves
The Linden
Tree of life screams
A Bird's shrill screech
A child's cry in his sleep"

. . .

"In the branches, death
Cherubim
With small faces
Cross their iridescent wings
Hop higher up in the trees . . . "

—from "Tree of Life" by Marie Luise Kaschnitz

CONTENTS

THREE

ACKNOWLEDGEMENTS

The author extends gracious thanks to the following journals where these poems first appeared:

Artemis: "Late Bees" | *Better Than Starbucks:* "Still Open" | *Burnt Pine Magazine:* "Marsh Violets" | *CCAR, The Reform Jewish Quarterly:* "Margot Again," "My Grandmother's Waltz," and "Aerie" | CDC Poetry Project: "Raccoon Latrine" | *Cirque:* "Lifeboat" | *Comstock Review:* "Who Flocks to the Sun?" | *Herstory:* "The Calculus of Rain" and "Children of the Cupola" | *Jewish Journal:* "An Uncensored Voice" | *Miller's Pond:* "With Each New Moon" | *Pact Press, We Refugees Anthology:* "Chalice" | *Piltdown Review:* "Poultry Shears" | *Raven Chronicles:* "Rabid Dog" | *Remembered Arts Journal:* "Headwind" | *Shirim:* "The Truth about Our American Births" | *South Florida Poetry Review:* "The Biters" | *Sou'wester:* "The Terrible Fate of Being a Child" | *Switched-On Gutenberg:* "The Deeps" | *Tar River Poetry:* "Can Believe In" | *Threepenny Review:* "The Ventriloquist" | *Well Review:* "Glacial Till" | *What Rough Beast, Indolent Press:* "A Daughter Returns," "And not to remember too much," and "Burlesque"

"Perhaps" and "Madrigal" are reprinted from *The Dreamer's Anthology: Writing Inspired by the lives of Dr. Martin Luther King Jr. and Anne Frank*

"Goddess Justitia" reprinted from *Poeming Pigeon*, The Poetry Box

"Christmas, 2004" appeared in Poetry on the Bus Project, Seattle

"Boogie Woogie" and "Blue Note" reprinted from *Sweetbrier*, Blue Begonia Press

Thanks to my colleagues in writing and the arts—Robin Arnitz, Christianne Balk, Irene Bloom, Erika Carter, Eileen Duncan, Carol Kelly, Tina Kelley, Susan Lane, Barbara Molloy, Anne Pitkin, Diane Ray, Mary Ellen Talley, Ruthie V., and Lillo Way

ONE

MY GRANDMOTHER'S WALTZ

One breast gone, her soft arms doughy, raised
above her head, no longer a woman,
she danced in torn slippers, her hair short-cropped.

One two three, one two three. And we, *die kinder,*
were of one mind in our jury as children:
we had, in our infinite power

made her into a kind of a contraption—
a Babushka spinning in its own squat body.
Always the counting beneath whistles of trains

running westward from the town of no money.
Always the wheeze of a breathy laughter
following its own spittle around the rheumy

house, which was half of a house. In the foyer
she blessed us with three quick spits on our heads.
Large flowers splattered a shift held together

with safety pins. Wooden floors she twirled
were scarred with nails. How could she be happy?
We made her smile, late afternoons, doilies seeded,

yellowed with age. The sun crept away,
the last train left as Bartok began again,
piano baring monstrous teeth. *One two three,*

one two three, one arm wound around my brother,
the other held out to me, she danced
to her own songs—accompanied gutturals.

So what if Poland wept for her blued
eyes, the cataract of mountains rearranging
what was once home before the flatlands.

How had we concocted this underling?
What could we do to send her back upstairs
to the room of garments, mothballed, hanging.

There, a hundred netted hats waited for her.
Like persons with no faces they loved to watch
five languages wound upside-down together

as she read Agatha Christie in Polish,
pausing only to extract a piece of green
from the thin mouth unlipsticked, sheepish

almost in its shy smile as another roast burned
in the oven, and we went free to giggle
and climb in her orchard. There, apples, stunted

by fear of heights would give a little
sour from their crabs, thrill the sky with danger,
make unleavened earth eat its own gristle.

Thin sun on daffodils.
Cup raised to the absent dreams of night.
Groundskeeper goes about his reversals.
Moss usurps patio stones, twigs cover
over this place where grief—
the salt-taste of grief, lies submerged in spring.

Tamp it down, push it back, keep it at bay.
You are only leaving the place you came to love.
You the one refugee, immigrant, emigrant
who never came to find a home
in any of the myriad houses
you occupied. You with your orange-teas
and cups of half-drunk milk,
pills laid out in ovals on odalisque-shaped bars.

Your greening willow gone,
and the fireflies, for whom the sun
was just a small bulb attached
to one part of the body.

That it could come and go at will,
that childhood would never end, and,
with it, the hot scalding tears
flowing after a beating, a reprimand, an accident
of jumping the fence to palm a shard of glass.

AERIE

This nest floats
on webs of light and dark
against a backdrop
of Jacob's Ladder, Lavender,
and Scotch Broom.

A stronghold
to house the young
with wisps of flagrant straw
against flutes of air,
and the dotted aprons

of well-meaning matriarchs
who would do better
to fold up their step stools
and go back
into the kitchen.

I continue
to stare at the sun
that blinds me,
a third-generation
German Jew borne

into the spattered walls
of a ghetto
broken by what brought it
brought together—those who
lofted themselves

with acrobatic stunts
and the somersaults
of imagination
from Munich
and the gas.

RACCOON LATRINE

The ringed beasts come
as if society were docile,
one by one up the trunk,
and where it splits—

that crotch where the squirrel
made his home—they squat
and do their business.
Markings on fur seem an entitlement

by moon-light: black-beige-gray.
As if a tiger had sold its stripes
for the right to be transgender
and own an opposable thumb.

They seem to sense, science-based
as do climbers, the outline of the yard,
its jig saw map from paving stones
to dead lilac, ringed

with marsh violets where, beneath the earth,
Persephone clenches her fingers
gone purple with the cold.
My husband rents a cage

as big as a double-wide.
He places a dry sandwich
far back where a door sits
propped open. Faces the trap

toward the house. Then, as if evidence-based,
two days into a week's rent,
he turns it toward the fence
as if privacy were a commodity

valued by the diversity
of the hungry.
Holly branches sway jauntily
across the wires. When I see

a fetus, its red berries and thorn-sharp leaves,
I remember being vulnerable
to chronic fatigue, sickness and pain.
Two daughters left for good.

Gone as well: the son who would
see these piles of black on bark,
smell the wakeful stink
and know just what to say.

"... the sea whose crescent blade cuts off
the dynasty of absurd griefs."
—Rene Char, "The Shark and the Gull"

Tonight I saw the three ghosts—
Leah and Israel and Jake
sitting together on the hard benches

of the Chetzemoka,
raising their glasses as they used to do,
laughing, talking, and interrupting one another.

Leah said, *One can always hope.*
Israel said nothing.
Jake's glass shook as he said *L'chaim.*

On board the Chetzemoka,
bleached hull, faded, rusted scrap of a boat
useless as Leah's lungs

these three pilgrims fast in their places.
They trust in the certainty of rescue,
old Jews, eternal optimists.

Israel's round bald head bobs up and down like a buoy.
For whatever misfortune landed them here
on the seats of the Chetzemoka
they blame no one.

THE DEEPS

We steer away from them.
There a sister or a cousin.
Here a tooth bobbing in a dream.
Possums plunder plums.
We sit at the helm with cocktails.
Steerage in the cargo bay.
A portion of amnesia.
The water plays at waves.
Perhaps it's only physics.
Concentric rings smell of fish.
We steer the craft as given.
Time in dry dock equals waste.
Sweet peas only grow at night,
when half-wild animals
pour from sewer grates.

EATING TONGUE

Nights they served tongue I kept to myself,
nothing unusual for a bookworm. Sat at the table,
saw circlets of lace crocheted together by the hook

once tucked away in a purse. Nights I didn't eat tongue
the sauce seemed thicker, creamy, at least a pound of butter
stirred into the roux. Nights they served the calves' tongue

I kept my thoughts inside my head where they rightly
belonged, or so I thought, until a knife
came from the sideboard, and someone's hand on it,

and then the slivers falling away, smaller at the tip,
thicker as the middle got past or was gotten past.
Then the old stories began to be told again,

as if it weren't tongue being served but some other organ—
the liver, the heart, the pipicles, which were, as we knew,
the chicken's belly buttons and therefore special

as they floated like little dicks to the top of the soup.
Mostly we knew everything, as all children know.
How to laugh, get tickled, go under the table

if such a rouse became necessary. Our hiding places
included closets, rooms behind rooms, rooms above rooms,
and the attic where the wasps lived in the wall.

We could feel them by putting our hands
against their nest—large as a bay of hale. 10,000 strong.
Stingers singing, bodies buzzing with electricity.

BLACK NIGHT

A faltering sun
spinning around earth
as if Galileo were wrong.
For punishment,
the drunk you live with.
The tree decorated,
gifts of Magi apportioned
beneath artificial boughs
laden with ornaments
they gave you when you let go
of their menorah,
stopped thinking
only one king could rule.
Come sleep beneath twinkle lights.
Watch juncos perch—
leaden skies above,
snowy white below.
No snow falls here.
You can barely make out what it is
the marrow clings to
in order to gild its bone.

DOWN THE SPREE

The German countryside does not lament.
It keeps an arbor of green for those who watch,
from the center of a river, for young girls
hanging laundry on lines. For the cheese
draining whey through a net bag. These houses
where long ago a resistance entered stone steps
down into rooms with damp walls,
where nothing happened except wind and water,
sturm und drang. Those taken hostage
in their pajamas merely agreed to board
trains and sit in straw. With the innocence
of childhood a river boat winds a string
between two banks. In the cabin below deck
emissaries spread caviar and *fois gras,* moisten
their lips with champagne. A hound's tooth scarf
decorates the neck of a Madame Directress
charged with the child who will or will not be gassed.

With Each New Moon

after René Char

A crescent hangs above mountains tinged with late-evening
sun.
A bright wing counters the despair of those who leave their
    dwellings
to become panhandlers on streets filled with cars whose drivers
inhabit a private music. Its reed-blade stems insufficiency.
    For those
who depart, nomadic, the desert sands equal waves of wind
beneath swaybacked horses. Worn saddlebags tear fur.
The night darkens and groans with hunger's iconic animals—
lion, hyena, jackal. Yet, for the refugee, each new moon
signals what can be felt but not believed: that every beginning
mirrors the largesse of a sun turning its face upon countries
    of forced emigration.
Of water running underground in its hidden labyrinth from
    spring
to spring with the lightness of fire, and the terrible children
laughing their way up from many floors below.

IN THE BLACK FOREST

As in a German fairy tale,
the trees dark
and widely spaced,
the forest floor well-swept

by a cretin.
Near the Avenue of Lindens,
close to a Holocaust memorial,
we walked.

The Spree, a ribbon of silver
ground down each day by hulls and sails—
this river proved, by tint and shade,
that water was a foil

and land a grave.
Each day cranes made the city
well or ill. Trams drained people
from stations and filled them up again.

Museums and churches
were fertile grounds for thought,
but not the forest. There
I wore my Gabardine and still was cold.

How much do you remember?
Each tree held a plaque with a number.
We joked about the Germans,
their need for order.

No underbrush.
The cretin kept well out of view,
his broom always poised at the threshold
of the next fork in the story.

We posed in monotone.
What was left of our intimacy
followed, like bread crumbs,
the path that led to a prison.

There we dreamt we were well fed,
that what we kept back from one another
couldn't be told apart
from what we surrendered.

The drudgery of a house.
Shadows come to tell of supper.
Pan full of grease in water, sloughing.
Bits of egg collect in the drain, yellow.
Hardened is the name of woman.
All hands and arms.
Hangnails come to tell.
Chores for the charwoman.
See her bend into soap.
Lean away from leisure.
In her stained rag a map of the world.
Countries never seen.
Meals brought by uniformed servants.
The silken, inner layers of a word called *pretty.*
Paired with white or red?
Once they asked that.
Once in the charcuterie she purchased veal.
Carried the butchered animal over cobblestones.
Her Achilles heal burned.
A time of injury.
As in times of peace one hears of wars.

The Snow Falls Silent as a God

Sisters I think of you alone,
each in a snow globe.
One mourns her lost dog, one makes preparations
for a journey abroad.
Another hovers above boxes
of her passed-on mother's vases,
planters, pots, and pans. She makes piles
of what to keep and what to throw away.

The white sky's fixed
beyond those firs
where I played with my siblings.
We harnessed a horse,
made an island
with a harbor and inlets of moss.

Sisters, watch the snow thicken
until it avalanches down slopes of Christmas trees
as if this were a village in the Alps.
Where are the pretty lights and fêtes?
Mourn with me, remember me, think
to yourselves how hope lived for a month
once, groping its way towards the solstice.

LATE BEES

Come for sweetness
when summer lies dying
in the brown yards

I remember the afternoon
two got caught in my shirt
and stung my breasts

Another year running
through Appalachian forest
three hornets stung my lips

September days
Mars setting in the east
as the red god of war

I hear school children at recess
recall my son who told
me of hiding in a corner

These hover over meat
or above Queen Anne's lace
dried centers browning

What other memory burns
like a coin you lost
with your youth

What other waspish souls gleam
just out of reach
like hummingbirds at a red plastic feeder

Sugar water
runs out through the jar
placed by a widow on a hook

Late bees enter the house
through a torn screen
because danger appeals most to those

bred on chaos whose parents came
to a strange country out of season
out of change

"Continues at a dog-trot each day going north..."
—Jack Gilbert

How praiseworthy, to be a train
full of people with dark eyes,
hands holding baskets and visors,
soot in the nail beds, all these bodies
sitting erect, and the few who stand
due to a lack of seats. Even the seats,
stained and worn, have not given out

yet. Vinyl sags at the edges,
the *tussah* seated where it sits always,
in the center. How splendid to be a train
full of plans and maps, of minds
in whose labyrinthine gray matter
the other languages hobble this way
and that, come from dozing,

go back to sleep, waken suddenly
as from a dream. A girl plays
at being grown up, a woman toys
with being a girl. The men, plural
always, horde whatever pesos accumulate
in their pockets, keep their elbows
close in. Such stoic chests. The blush

of a marionette on the girl's cheek,
of powder on the woman. However
close or far from home, the quick
rubs against skin, thirst begins at the back
of the throat and inches forward
until all the cars in this string—
carriages replete with names

riding on steel wheels and tracks—
remember how thirsty travel is.
How little distance has been accomplished
by the machinations of the conductor
checking tickets made out of paper.
Leaving in his wake that shushing
as after a war.

PERHAPS

after Sandor Csoori

You too were a leper of the feelings.
One who had to be cut off in order
to survive the sister who beat her head
against the wall on weekends, especially
Sunday evenings before she was returned
to the convent.

What tree grew to block the front window
and hide the inner workings of that house?
First you root clippings of quaking aspen
in a bucket of water,
then the transfer to dirt,
still the happiness you wished for dies.

It could be the train carries
the amputated memory of its caboose
what with the loud wail of this whistle
echoing off the grange, the bar, the silo.

What isn't seen or heard doesn't exist
in these kinds of forests,
only purple-headed flowers.
Those change to mysterious heads
of white, as if that too
were a kind of blossom
known to aridity, heat, and blight.

Harbor the red light blinking on the wing
outside the porthole in the dark
the memory of birdsong
think you may yet be heir to the earth

Titmouse wren hare and squirrel find their way
hold the fields tightly
in the grip of daydream
you who never sleep on planes

Pronounce your name
though no one asks
anonymous stranger passing from east to west
remember the muscled thighs

the six pack of a god who
despite strength presses on the same stone
up and upward climbs
finding no place to rest

Tumble on through the dark
towards a city you hold fast to
as an exile keeps her memory trained
on mountains and sea

Take your mind farther down the map
where deer nod off in long grass
and cattails nudge
the vanishing point you call *home*

TWO

GODDESS JUSTITIA

I met her out walking near a lake.
The lake held Narcissus's strangled hands.
A childlike song came from her mouth.

After all, the scales were light,
and hung from her hands
like mittens threaded through a coat.

She wanted to see the sun
fall into the water as a minted coin,
to hear the crows overhead flying ragged

towards their place of rest.
The rape of so many women—
how could you keep silent,

I asked. *The circumcision of female children.*
I was blindfolded, she whispered in my ear
near the madrona where our paths crossed.

THE BITERS

They come from corners,
those younger sisters
who envy the older one
and plant their marks
on inner arms—
half circles almost breaking skin.
The savagery of sisterhood,
its secret rites and rituals.
The bitten one, the one
who bites. Which comes first—
kinship or jealousy?
What form does rage take
in those not yet civilized
whose anger flares and digs
its insignias in the softest parts—
flesh and memory.
What of the erotic zones
sisters share, when they tickle
one another, or seem to take
one under the other's wing?

WHO FLOCKS TO THE SUN?

Wizened, they board planes to the south,
carrying and hauling, jacketed
and sunglassed, limping down the aisles.

Mica shines from granite. Surely a glint
will find an eye, the fist grasp its cocktail
like first love. The Joshua Tree needs

little to hover over sand, the Pipe Organ
Cactus plays a requiem of survival,
roses not made of petals line the drives,

cerulean skies above black mountains
darken only for stars. In a desert
the shade shelters beneath rocks. Perhaps

the rattlesnake will deliver poison
to end the foolishness of longevity—
life after life's bequeathed to daughter

and son, to granddaughter and grandson,
great and greater treasures, precious riches.
O purple majesty, o pathetic walker,

how many birds make a mass, a crowd,
a throng? Who is it feeds, rests, travels
alone surrounded by their herd?

THE WISE MAN

My mother laughs when I ask
where she took her mother's
just-plucked chicken to be declared kosher—
oh he was just a neighbor across the street,
nothing special, I really don't remember.

Her stories belie secret wounds.
Why, before cooking dinner, did my *Bobbie*
wrap the just-plucked bird in newspaper
and ask her daughter to trot
around sooty tenements of Montreal
to ask whether it could be eaten?

I ask about the pronouncement
spoken by this person, wizened
in my imagination, a man like a toothpick
sprouting legs and arms,
gesticulating in his run-down room
over a salmonella-breeding hunk of flesh.
If there was blood, if the egg remained
stuck in its cavity . . . if the pipicle . . .

I remember the foyer
where, forced to enter,
we endured the spittle of a gnome,
our Bubba, a neutered woman
who laughed and waltzed and cried.

According to another story
the red beads around her neck
protect us from the evil eye.
Yet the child knows its own head
from a cabbage.
The child's limbic door
swings open on a busted hinge.

RUMBLE SEAT

Not that I mind riding
these stories of the past,
bumping along into the country
with the cousins and uncles,
a bit of dirt kicked up
to lather my face.

Not that I mind hearing
the same stories over
and again, their nuance
finally clear as the streams
where they first festered
and began to own their lives
as we cannot.

Do me a favor, you
up there in front—
go on driving slowly
past cows whose udders
sweep the grass, past
willows and cypresses
the color of sun on rust.

Keep talking while I rest
a little longer
at the beginning of a fairy tale.
The milk has its head
of cream and comes
in green glass, the newspaper
riffles its own pages
in the wind.

Let my mother
be young again,
courted by men who want to take her
away from my father,
his new body strong
as this one taken
from the guts of an engine.

CAN'T RETURN

Firs rise in green skirts
before the window.
Can't go back, the wind
says in its all too human moan.

I feel the degenerate within
take more of what it owns—
this flesh house
where all winter I sheltered.

Can't return the little birds
skewered and gnashed,
nor the sun
burning away wisps of fog.

How green the green
on February grasses,
how bright the whites
of branches tipped with sun.

The shadow grew like a wing.
Can't return the sturdy log
of a toddler I swaddled,
its baby's breath dried to tinder.

MADRIGAL

Strict birds come from the trees.
I remember a word you said.
Swallows come in two's, jays in threes.

I grieve only so much for the dead.
We have made a language of hurt,
where old fathers lie in bloodied lead.

There the ephemeral maids feign, apart
from all theater, red-cheeked happiness.
I recall the day you once broke my heart.

Swallow hard, believe in twoness,
that three makes a crowd.
Admit you hold the sister, you obsess

as strict birds fly from their nunneries
in the trees. The jays blue, swallows spotted.
I who forgive cannot forget. Grief

plies my body, a sad hound shouldered
in scarves hound's tooth patterned.
I remember a word you said.

Lost all his teeth by the age of forty,
according to legend. Chased his wife
around with a kitchen knife
As memory searches the gray banks
it takes down the patriarchy.

It was she who chased him—Bubba,
the educated woman of Poland—
a rarity, a blemish on his conscience
as he praised with his sweet voice
the feminine idol who existed nowhere
in the flatlands, to whom
he returned each evening.

The charred roast still in the oven,
no one minding the children,
and Bubba upstairs reading
Agatha Christies in five languages.
Firing the house cleaner who stole
silver from the humble house,
offering favoritism to her last born son,
the only skinny one, as dessert.

I see my father, the weakling,
teased for his name, for glasses:
Oscar four eyes. I see the pen
he wrapped in newspaper
to give as a gift to a friend.
Theirs an arranged marriage—
she couldn't cook or clean nor receive
guests who came for counsel,
solace, to celebrate high holidays.

His voice still projects to the back
of the small Winnipeg synagogue
where he, the holy man, lives
to yodel, albeit humbly,
the blessings of his single god,
Creator of the Universe, Amen.

In Montreal

Maybe tonight the mattress
won't list to one side.
I'll check the clock, remove my diamonds.
take a couple of pills.

Downstairs the men
will be playing a game of Kabala,
talking mysticism, arguing,
downing the teetotaler's glass.

Its blue rim shines in the bathroom,
where water's overflowed the bathtub,
rippled along the carpet.
How much will they pay for my bitterness?

Misogyny aside,
would they use bills, moldings,
toast and jelly? How stop the river
caused by bad plumbing

or improvident contractor—
the One Who never thought
how much it would cost
to shut a woman up?

POLISH MOTHER

She speaks six languages,
leans into the kitchen
where memory concocts sweet cakes,
poppy seed triangles, egg matzos.

She lights the apple orchard
with a lamp called *moon*
and then goes to bed
in a dirty housedress.

While she sleeps
her children swing
from branches into nightmare.
They dream of falling

from great heights, sailing
across deep waters
to no harbor. They see black spots
that resemble spiders

crawling along crib bars,
hunt for cold fish in soupy waters.
Under what reproof
did her long dark hair

vanish beneath its synagogue covering?
In family legend,
near a snow-capped mountain
in Delatyn, between two wars,

coins sang in her handkerchief.
She wore a woolen dress
to work in the office of her father
the notary, who taught her

against custom to read and write.
Dowry-worthy at sixteen,
marriage arranged with an officer
of the first world war,

now she spits three times
on the heads of her children's children
zpt zpt zpt—
to keep away the evil eye.

A glass swan
has let itself in to the room
where Bess plays the Boogie Woogie,
her plump white hands
passing over the keys.

Only Bess could spread the octaves
and bring them together again.
By this I mean she knew how to sew
the highs to the lows,
even without lessons.

The train must be passing
close to this house. Some
relationship exists between
the swan and the train
although it is sordid, no doubt,

created by the matchmaker
who, disguised as a yenta,
inadvertently brought the two quantities
together, the one entirely
symbolic, and the other so punctual

it could only be real.
On Bess's ring finger
there would have been gold,
if Ida had ever taught her
the facts of life. These I heard

she learned in her twenties, from magazines.
Stranger still, Ida didn't know
where babies come from
after four pregnancies. Though from
Agatha Christie's, she knew

how to follow the trail of the murderer
out of the bedroom and into
the living room, how to pick up
hairs and threads from a rug
embedded with wool flowers.

If the train is patriarchal
it would oppose the swan,
which by now has grafted itself
to the top
of the cake dish.

If Bess were to be married
she'd have to overcome the conditions
of ignorance. After which nothing
can be said, except to make
certain allusions—

to the monstrous piano sitting in the room
with its mouthful of keys,
to the swan that has no doubt
been sitting a long time
on top of a cake the goyim

would have found
too dense, its spongy layers
marbled with darks and lights.
The faint taste of a liqueur,
not rum but more exotic,

and sweetness, the kind
that surpasses even the expectations
of childhood. A girl could eat
this cake and shrink or grow.
The aromatic substances

in Bess and Ida's house were dressed
with oil or grease, covered
by the excesses of memory,
as hurt can be liquored up sometimes
but still remains a drug, watery.

That would account for the train
if not for its percussion,
a whistle passing too close
to the tiny yard trimmed
by geometry to the size

and shape of a triangle.
If I pay attention to the train's
whistle I hear certain undertones,
men and boys, or, in the rumbling
tons of metal

those Holocaust stories told
and later taken back,
as the most difficult facts
come to be handled by time
and distance.

Mother's come home
with a bundle of flannel,
another red-faced doll propped
in the corner.

It shrieks for solace like old man
trapped in a stocky body,
arms and bow legs waving
at thin air. At the zenith

for one weightless second
the old woman this baby was named after
limps from a pocket of limbo
into a poor version

of the afterlife. Chava Tzeitzel: Chava, Eva, Eve, Judith?
Bubba's bubba pinches my cheeks,
adjusts the red bandana
that makes her head a winter cabbage.

Another sister is born. Et-tel-bela—
Esther, Ethel, Elaine, Ruth Elinor?
With the blond curls and blue eyes
of a traitor, hurried into a glass

incubator, this preemie gulps air,
fishnet covering thin skin. Mother,
napping, lets me feed my baby brother,
who burps and hiccups like the alcoholic

he was named for: Shalom-ov-Rom.
Saul, Samuel, Joel? Joel Harvey?
Having Americanized the names
of the newly dead,

Mother and Father
smile shyly at one another,
hold hands in the car,
decide to become citizens.

Metal handles, large, the scissor
for a thigh or a wing, when feathers flew up,
sank like wishes, settled on dirty floors.
Her fingers looped, her mouth set,
she lays into the bird. A pale thing, that,
hardly bloody but for the bone's center,
where, once separated from the body,
a little fluid leaks on newsprint.
Nothing wasted—the gizzard boiled,
liver sizzling in a fry pan—even the neck—
her teeth chew strands of meat.
The best there is, she says, grinning
a meat-toothed smile like a child,
Nothing automatic about the parts,
or the anatomy of memory. Seasonings
thrown with fingertips, no spoons to measure with.
The extraneous gone, only the killing of it
left to be explained. *I remember they'd run
around after their heads were cut off.*
Leaning in, butcher's apron fastened
around a large waist. Not a doter, nor a worrier.
Her father killed the bird, her mother taught
fingers. The piano didn't take. Hugs
the wooden block that holds (an actor
should come on scene only when crises loom)
the chicken's fate—its marriage to water,
onion, carrots, knaidlach, schmaltz.

CHRISTMAS, 2004

It's true the sampan lanterns
      twinkle on the water
like Venetian gold.

My son knew a man in Thailand
      who ferried he and his friend
from night to night
      before a big wave
swept his lined face and little boat away.

BOOGIE WOOGIE

As if there were,
in the pentagonal shape
of the family, a reason
for the Boogie Woogie,
For Mother's mouth chewing,

her bird motions,
her story of the wise man
in the tenement building
who would bless a chicken.
Bess' stodgy fingers moved across

the piano's smile,
Ida swayed over the wooden
floor in her stubborn waltz,
her house dress held closed
by safety pins, her missing breast.

Snow pinned cafe curtains
to oriental wallpaper, salt
spattered Ida's glasses,
Mother dropped a stitch.
We clasped gray hands,

ate hard crackers, opened the jar
with its allotment of air.
I remember Mother's pattern changed
while she knit. Six-foot drifts
printed with angels

bordered northern streets,
tzimmis and carrots
made an argyle of winter.
Quarter tones bent the edge of dirt
until sickness and want peeled back.

Ida's glasses, spattered
with grease and tears—
Sid would hold them over
the sink and rinse, then step
back, wiping his hands on shirt tails.

In the orchard out back
one stunted crabapple poked
from the ground
next to what was soft
and had fallen.

Never wore gold
nor women
with dyed hair
who'd tuck an arm
to vine the sleeve
of an Armani suit.
Didn't sport chains
against chests
whose hair showed
a bit for us children,
just to titillate.

Yet the hoity toity,
when we sat at table
to break bread
and snicker snacker,
turned to one another
over our heads
when they spoke
of the great unwashed masses,
their tailored shoulders
shaking with laughter.
Players growing ash
and waitresses
bringing seconds
of prime rib.

We the butt
of jokes and tickles.
Until, outside in air
so fresh you could live on it,

the buttercup game
played beneath
our chins—*do you like
butter?* Who'd fall
for fat, become one
of theirs, with breasts
called *knockers,*
when the grease kicked in?

THREE

CHILDREN OF THE CUPOLA

Cliché to say they're gone, wings pinned
behind supple backs, longings fled
with the Stellar Jays' flitting from porch to branch.

Random pleasures in the grass, and me
just one of two thousand, when a childhood
of interminable duration played out

in greenish evil. *Time is old but not large,*
the Hebrew poet said. I feel them lift
one by one, ghost prints pressed between rollers

and the glittering of hubris taken too,
along with a hot southern night, a virgin pina colada,
nests of roots, and the pelican's gullet.

Trite to add the stars, their manifest—
old light, storied halos. I see others approach
to climb on shoulders, ringing in new-born eternity.

Bubbe, let bells and chimes reach your ear.
Broadcast shrieks and alms—fuming stones of an ancient city,
mere evaporate rising, arising in wide time.

MARGOT AGAIN

Wearing those clothes from the old country,
unwashed, no make up,
a cousin I must humor.
Let me make you some chicken soup—
she takes over the kitchen
in one two three time. Chops on the board,
stirs leeks into a paste
of schmaltz and onions.
I tell her—you've brought back
a case of nerves, you must go.
I beseech you—take the train, call a car,
go back to that town in Europe,
a village so small it doesn't exist.
She turns and says
What is it about you?
You don't know how to enjoy a hearty meal?
You race against the clock that beats
with the sound of hooves on a track.
Always betting on the wrong horse,
Pain in a Pocket.

DAHLIAS

After they began to crowd
the field with their names
they formed cliques,
resisted impressionism
and the aesthete.
They were not commoners,
not cousin nor kin.

Even after the fork
earned its tines
and the yearling left
for another pasture
they went on blooming
long into October,
throwing out buds—
spider-shut wads
that would open
spiky, thick-lidded petals.

As if to go against the grain—
to flaunt their umbrage
at the season.
Saber-edged fluff
now tow-headed,
now blonde, red-headed, brunette.
Cloudscape, A la Mode.

The tall ones, whorish,
leaned against the house
as if to prove the axiom
Fancy never tires of itself.

Inside the kitchen
the woman who fed them
on manure, who would turn
their white shallot-heads
in shallow graves
once they finished
dazzling ever-smaller crowds,
dried the last dish
and darkened the house.

THE TERRIBLE FATE OF BEING A CHILD

Carried from one bed to the next,
deposited beneath covers, expected
to sleep, hounded and scorned
and teased, fed one tidbit and another
and talked about in front of the others,
abandoned to third person,
all from not sleeping, which is,
as they all know, disappearing—
kin to dying—missing out on
barbed jokes thrown to the four corners
of rooms, skies, and greens, the croquet set
in waiting, its colored balls hidden
in plastic. You, the one they want
gone, there all along with no way
to escape the sun hovering
behind blankets, the false animals
in fake fur, and your leash tied
to the end of the world.

BURLESQUE

January—pale month in a reliquary.
Planted in soil, iced over, snowed upon.
A moon, lamp-like, hung
above the garden behind cloud cover.

The titmouse, the sparrows,
moving like insects over these grounds.
An almost monstrous lack, informed
by cold, hunger, and neglect.

Will the willow pirouette tonight,
its branches scraped clean of tear-shaped leaves?
The deer made out of twine falls
on its side in the realtor's yard.

Nothing risqué but death. No ragtime
but alcohol. At the party
guests sit like actors in a sitcom on a TV flat screen.
A woman with a drink in her hand, like Gypsy Rose Lee.

Cold concocts its smallish, shortest song.
No sun in the body
when moss presides in the garden.
I dreamt of RSVP's,

nodes on the lilac, tumor
in the bark of the apple,
an absence of buds, which is to say,
when did the operetta become an affair?

MARSH VIOLETS

You want them to go on
blooming in the rain, the cold sleet
sheeting down from whatever clouds
pass overhead, bringing news of dark omens.

You wish for spring when you see
filigree petals springing from moss
below the oak, its doubled trunk
that became a raccoon latrine last winter.

Though they open like doilies
the flower isn't so fragile, the stem
hard to punch through with thumb
and index finger. Picking them

makes you want to think it's spring—
some potion like a salve or balm
hovers in the air. The weather still
changeable, the sun stolen from the zenith

by storm. As if Juno's chariot were unsteady,
his reins held in the hands of a child god
who thought he was more immortal
than a peacock. You got what you prayed for.

Yes, punishment came with the granting
of the prayer-wish. You begin to think green
more indecent than purple. That the erotic
dreams are less credible than these flowers.

Which is to say, the wind screams
above itself about masochism, sadism,
and all the shades between.
You knew a perpetual winter

came with your last bleed. That sterility
would equal a certain dryness in the humors.
Perhaps the keratinous body you inhabit
now is your *soul*—that word so precious

in youth—whatever it is that still seethes
with life's precocious mysteries. Like blue-
eyed girls who behave miserably
at bedtime, and these clumps

self-seeding a circle around the base
of the raccoon latrine. As coldly unaware
as those raccoons who lumber
across violets, one at a time all night long.

THE VENTRILOQUIST

Later, when the voice in his belly
is not loud enough to make him
sick, he explains to the grass and trees
how she wouldn't go away.

Sleep was a problem for her.
She wore a kerchief
and spoke Greek,
her apron always spattered

with ink from irises.
Whenever purples grow too heavy
and topple over
he feels less like a prophet.

Her mop of curls, her broomstick legs,
it's not that he misses her simple body
made of wood. Nor does he think
analysis could cure

her complaints, nor stop the adrenalin
that flowed between them continuously
as attention. A summer
more ragged than pretty,

and he's popping up like a cork
from the dusty water
of her drowning
to the surface of his sheets.

Glacial Till

They live on ground so hard
it's impossible to plant a tree.
The scrape of shovel against rock
is enough to make a grown man cry.

Once he turned up a crop of stones
and came to her
saying they were potatoes.
He swore they would never go hungry again.

Once she cut a sunflower down
in its prime
and he was blind with rage for days.
You wouldn't want them to visit,

these caricatures of Adam and Eve—
the woman wily in her weakness,
the man stupid in his strength.
The hill, as it erodes,

brings them gifts
as if took pity on their state.
Last year the armor of a cyton.
This week the leaves of a fern

pressed between pages of slate.
They are beginning to recognize
their own story in shells
and bird bones.

The Dream of Punishment

We carry our papers in slots of mouths
as we rise on a glass escalator
to the mesa where we'll be sentenced.
Green cards, passports, visa's. The god—
a man with a cane—decides
how long each one will stay prone
in crucifixion position, staring up
at a sky made of marble and ice.
I jaw the cardboard, wait my turn
among this horde of folksy grown ups
fettered to the state. Conscripted from house,
trailer, igloo, terraced fields of rice.

STILL OPEN

after Marie Luise Kaschnitz

In the July yard,
a sear of dun grass,
certain buttercups raise
yellow upside down umbrellas
as if to you,
who died in 1974.

I hunt and peck
for words to call this world,
try to gather strength
from your curiosity.

An admirable trait
imaginable only to those Lilliputians
who met Gulliver
when he stepped ashore.
After trying to subdue him
they returned
to their kitchens
where you waited in silence
disguised as a placid mother
or an honorable guest.

I never liked men,
preferred to be alone
with the window dressing,
to sit with my back against what was left
of the forest
eating a salad of green leaves,
at the table old roses.

A Daughter Returns

Brown nose in the blackberry flowers of June
muscled flanks
lifted forefoot curves the ribs move beneath fur

Trees in green wedding gowns hide her angry father
birds dirge their only trill
over and again in the age of guns and mass shootings

In the short time I watch she's worked her way
half across the yard driven by hunger
lifting each weed like a cross toward the white sky

that may symbolize purity
I see the grave the abscess the sinkhole
where she fell after the change

Scree eases its stones across the rocky lip that hides Snow Lake
where swans of frost glide Berlin rivers
and skaters wearing yarn coats clasp hands in pas de deux

The girl-woman breaks away
twirls the second smallest matryoshka from its wood
Before she disappears it is essential

to capture the ritual of grooming
the way our brown eyes met across a distance of old glass
forged from Santorini sand

and our mutual awareness of predation by men

THE CALCULUS OF RAIN

Come to drum this metal roof in sixteenth
and thirty-second notes, to puddle, gouge
a dirt road that spins the tires' worn teeth.
There you once pulled into a large garage
and felt at home. But then came age
and forsythia, the bush rabbits sift
to nibble yellow. Rain's the teacher's grounds.
Xeno's paradox, where half means half

x infinity—the tortoise's handicap
never allows the hare to win the race.
Splatter drops in my eye, vitreous
detachment, blood and debris. Hazard cups
the field of view, invents the calculus:
irrational, continuous.

Irrational, continuous—
the verge on which we stand to see the moon,
its cratered shell a self once benign,
then abandoned, imprisoned. Fingers
count to ten when little, then twenty—
learn with glee sets of nine, listen to Pi
till, forced to memorize the language
of numbers without knowing why,

turn their back on trigonometry.
Memories drip and pummel, the past returns
in dream: satin buttons forced through tight
holes, bodices of stiff sateen to hide
budding breasts. Mother knits and purls.
Her needles *clic clac* like the train to Prague.

Her needles *clic clac* like the train to Prague.
She sits and sips her glass of wine. Poor father's
slipped below the Hawthorne. His ashes beg
the mud for clues. Our sun's corona flares
as if to redeem its scientist, one who
took to house arrest still mumbling heresy.
Sir Newton fudged the rules of gravity.
An apple falls fast as a suicide—

is that you at the top of the falls,
unsure whether to leap? Nah, stay
awhile longer, what happens to the body
needn't concern its host. The four laws
of Buddhism precede each demise. Study
especially old age with its ailments.

Especially old age with its ailments
exponentially grown larger. A hole
in the body peels back, throws off the soul
only to find a burning flame, or its
equivalent: the nothing for whose crown
curious eyes seek and tongues wag, trade
in words. It's for the sake of dissolution
we were made. Tibetan monks draw with hard

colored chalks on boards, make elaborate
mandalas, then take them to the river
and convert the dust to milk. In that
way each comer receives a treasure
to remember: shaken colors gone brown at
last, intertwined, joining the common hub.

Lastly intertwine, join the common hub,
we girls who shy away from mathematics.
Even those professor-born, who lobbed
our balls into the grass of an artistic
court where money didn't matter, or so
we became convinced. Our collective wince
fills rivers and seas, as rain drops do.
The infinite falls collect in tins.

Give us the means to water our thirst
for knowledge. Must the heretic be thrown
overboard, the sky hold irrational bits?
Puzzle back the past, inhale present scents.
Father's physics rises from springs beneath,
come to drum this metal roof in sixteenths.

RABID DOG

When you wake me
I tend your stenosis
brush your bad mouth

I try to catch the happy fleas
bouncing up from bed sheets
where we sleep together

I pet and fondle those pretty stones
clustered around your neck
Swarovski crystals set in grape leather

Best friend of man
like a Berlin train with plush seats
you run on a timetable

Your presence fetters my ankles
although I honor in principle
the morals that keep me from leaving

Dog born of wolf I promise
in these new vows to try harder
to hear your infection

Listen to my hand absently petting
the bark the yip the howl the rage

The men will bet this evening
behind the coal miner's restaurant
with their green dollars.
Two birds—one squat and lithe,
the second large and square.
The manager of alley entertainments
is dirty with sweat.
His men sway and swear.
Women on these farms
rise before dawn.
Windows sparkle from inside
with humidity, flesh,
lamps, and frying eggs.
Bacon comes straight from heaven
to grease the talk of weather.
Another goat's born in the barn—
no need to rotate it
in the womb.
The first one's shoulder lodged,
leg stuck in a flamingo pose.
Apart from in-fighting
things turn out. Daughters
never lecture their mothers,
and sons sweeten with age.
When they leave,
no other country adopts
the boy to kill him with its war.

The cobblestone streets, parrots talking in shade,
a breeze off the ocean, bougainvillea vining trellises.

Los arcos—three rocks where whales breach.
Frigate birds, pelicans, and swifts buzz the pool,

coming in as if to land on the equipoise of water,
to stun the body back from its reliquary of secrets.

Nothing in that slow-motion film can be erased,
unstuck from the spiral kingdom of place.

The old injury carries its sting, a scorpion poised
above scar tissue, a boa holding the shroud of amnesia.

Moon as goldfish, as moth, or milk.
Anything but this scorched pink candy
waxing from half to full to lie open-
eyed as a beetle. Moon as sun, kin,
mirror, omen. Or any deity
perched on high. Not this crawling across
terrain gone dull with smoke's amnesia.
Noxious sky, now return the goose egg
stolen from a star that tried to teach
with tentacles of corona. Black spotted
moon, o moon-flower once borrowed,
due to be returned.

AN UNCENSORED VOICE

I was a guest in the province
of notes. Carrying my fiddle and bow
I walked down the avenue of heavy oaks.
It was the morning the children left home
for good. I passed soldiers and hostages,
came to a broad, whitewashed building
set on a gracious southern lawn.
An obsolete palace, home for lepers.
I listened to the nothing I'd been
and the nothing I'd done,
heard the scratching of leaves and birds,
small sisterly voices moved by wind.

A Crust of Snow

You like to imagine, as the drifts melt—
beached whales, pelican beaks,
royal penguins
stranded far from their eggs—
you the humanist
see human forms all too well.
A hand reaching from soot-remnants,
pleats and darts
folded back and tacked
as if to embroider a time
of angel-making,
when, hooded with your sisters
you fell back into virgin snow,
arms swinging back and forth.
Wings no longer taped,
no more straightjacketed to earth.

NOTES

The epigraph is from "Tree of Life" from *Selected Later Poems of Marie Luise Kaschnitz*, trans. Lisel Mueller, Princeton University Press, 1980.

"Lifeboat" is in memory of Leah and Israel Bloom, and Jacob Kastner.

René Char was a twentieth-century French poet and member of the French Resistance.

In "Eating Tongue," the word "pipicles" refers to an organ of the chicken.

"Sisters, The Snow Falls Silent as a God" was inspired by Edith Södergran.

In "Black Night," "one king" refers to a primary tenet of Judaism: the Hebrew God is portrayed as unitary and solitary.

"The Hoi Poloi" is an idiom meaning "the great unwashed masses."

In "The Rebbe, The Shatz," Rebbe means rabbi, especially a religious leader of the Hasidic sect. A shatz is a cantor or singer.

The word "tzimmis" in "Boogie Woogie" refers to a traditional Ashkenazi Jewish sweet stew made from carrots and dried fruits.

In "Polish Mother," the city of Delatyn, which is now Galicia, was the site of a Jewish massacre in 1941.

"Blue Note" and "Boogie Woogie" were written for and in memory of Elizabeth Kastner.

"Mama Vallone's" is titled after a restaurant in Cle Elum, Washington.

"A Crust of Snow" is dedicated to Ellen Katz and Marcy Laufer.

About the Author

JUDITH SKILLMAN is author of sixteen collections of poetry, including *Kafka's Shadow, House of Burnt Offerings*, and *The Phoenix: New & Selected Poems*. She is the recipient of an Eric Mathieu King Fund Award from the Academy of American Poets for her book *Storm* (Blue Begonia Press). Her poems have appeared in *Poetry, The Iowa Review, LitMag, Shenandoah, Prairie Schooner, Zyzzyva, We Refugees,* and numerous other journals and anthologies.

Ms. Skillman has been a Writer in Residence at the Centrum Foundation in Port Townsend, Washington. Her passion for collaborative translation can be seen in *Hawaii Review*'s poems of Macedonian poet Jovica Eternijan, and in the chapbook *Anne-Marie Derése in Translation & The Green Parrot* (Ahadada Books). Her work has been nominated for Pushcart Prizes, the UK Kit Award, Best of the Web, and is included in *Best Indie Verse of New England*.

— www.judithskillman.com

SHANTI ARTS

NATURE · ART · SPIRIT

Please visit us on online
to browse our entire book catalog,
including poetry collections and fiction,
books on travel, nature, healing, art,
photography, and more.

Also take a look at our highly
regarded art and literary journal,
Still Point Arts Quarterly, which
may be downloaded for free.

www.shantiarts.com

CPSIA information can be obtained
at www.ICGtesting.com
Printed in the USA
FSHW012356020520
69836FS